A Little Hard to Swallow:
1334

By

Lorin Morgan-Richards

Author of
"Why is Everyone Staring?" Etc.
A Raven Above Press
Studio City, CA
www.aravenabovepress.com

Paperback © 2016

ALL RIGHTS RESERVED

DEDICATED TO
ROZZ

All the Characters and Events portrayed in this
book are the creation of Lorin Morgan-Richards

Edited by Kevin Alan Richards

A RAVEN ABOVE PRESS PUBLICATION

ISBN 978-0-9973193-1-6

Please, if you will.
If your stomach's not too weak.
read along so I may share
a tale most bleak.

It is, by all means,
a very favorite sad suite.
Whose notes I dare say
I wish not repeat.

For there in a frame,
Pictured a dear ol' friend.
Who though I've never met
a life I need to amend.

Entered this world on flying ship,
Such as nothing before seen
if you blinked you missed
the arrival of this fiend.

Roger was he named,
Though why was not very clear
he was not jolly like the pirate
nor carrying a wooden spear.

But realizing in time,
what he would become
he began to see strangely
how this world was run.

Being raised in strictest discipline,
he entertained himself where he could,
mixing odd toys together
on a stage before a cross of wood.

He enjoyed his youth
listening to the new rage
painting and cut-ups
and dreaming of a life on stage.

Discovered did he a special place
 a cemetery down the road
 to sit quietly with thoughts
 away from suburban erode.

Blooming with funeral wreaths
reciting poems of stone
fondest of one named Rozz
which he took for his own.

Inspired he wrote
poems took form,
he saw himself a bringer of song
by fans in swarm.

A band without a name
would find on his friend's breast
there engraved were C and D
conceiving the words Christian Death.

An artist named Ron
shared his cause
truth now be revealed
for arts without applause.

Christian Death gained strength,
    the lineup evolved.
  Agnew, O', and Demone
 missing pieces were solved.

But all was not right,
the band split in two,
Rozz would marry,
formed a band of the coup.

Shadow Project was born
for eerie effects of bombs
they toured all of Europe
the home of Johannes Brahms.

But up and down Rozz faltered
chasing his dragon addiction
without the support of friends
never had he survived this affliction.

A Little Hard to Swallow: 1334

On he went to write
about the drug's sickly hold
with his friends
who collaborated and consoled.

The cards laid on the floor
　　focus soon left
　he was the tarot's fool
expiring a final breath.

Friends never forgot,
fans felt his pain,
ashes against the wind,
their hero was slain.

A life may end
Yet a name lives today
Stars may glimmer
A spirit never fades.

A flying ship came forth
shooting star's little hearse
collecting his spirit up
to tour the Universe.

www.ingramcontent.com/pod-product-compliance
Lightning Source LLC
Chambersburg PA
CBHW070554300426
44113CB00011B/1903